DANGEROUS JESUS
PARTICIPANT'S GUIDE

DANGEROUS JESUS

PARTICIPANT'S GUIDE

A six-session study
based on the book & video series

KEVIN "KB" BURGESS

TYNDALE
MOMENTUM®

A Tyndale nonfiction imprint

Visit Tyndale online at tyndale.com.

Visit Tyndale Momentum online at tyndalemomentum.com.

Tyndale, Tyndale's quill logo, *Tyndale Momentum*, and the Tyndale Momentum logo are registered trademarks of Tyndale House Ministries. Tyndale Momentum is a nonfiction imprint of Tyndale House Publishers, Carol Stream, Illinois.

Cover designed by Dean H. Renninger

Published in association with the literary agency of The Fedd Agency, Inc., P.O. Box 341973, Austin, TX 78734.

The author gratefully acknowledges Holly Crawshaw for her assistance in developing this manuscript.

For information about special discounts for bulk purchases, please contact Tyndale House Publishers at csresponse@tyndale.com, or call 1-855-277-9400.

Library of Congress Cataloging-in-Publication Data

A catalog record for this book is available from the Library of Congress.

ISBN 978-1-4964-8276-1

Printed in the United States of America

29	28	27	26	25	24	23
7	6	5	4	3	2	1

CONTENTS

A NOTE FROM KB

What do you think about when you hear the word *dangerous*?

Or maybe, more specifically, *who* do you think about?

I spent a lot of my life wanting to be dangerous. To me, being dangerous meant being someone whose presence commanded respect. Someone whose presence brought admiration, but maybe a little bit of fear too. Someone with influence. Someone with almost godlike status. Resources, power, and respect are hip-hop's holy trinity—and as a hip-hop artist, I wanted them all. That's what being dangerous looked like to me.

But the more I studied Jesus and the more I experienced Jesus, the more I realized that I was missing it—I was missing *Him*. Because no one has more resources than Jesus. No one has more power than Jesus. And no one deserves more respect. The Bible tells us that for Jesus *every* knee will bow and *every* tongue will confess that He alone is king. Not only does Jesus have resources, power, and respect, but if anybody else has them, it's because He's allowed it.

This Jesus is more powerful than the powers that once over-powered me. His hold on me is stronger than the strongholds that once held me. Everything and everyone in all of creation is influenced by Jesus. Jesus puts danger in danger.

What I've learned and I want you to see is that there is no one more dangerous than the Lord Jesus Christ.

This study is for anyone searching for the real Jesus, and for those who are growing weary, confused, and maybe even a little disillusioned by how He's misrepresented. And you should know up front—I don't come in peace. I come in hopes of tearing apart a construct of Jesus that's not only inaccurate but destructive.

I come in hopes of recasting Christianity in a culture of knock-offs where we've become so accustomed to the counterfeit that the real thing sounds like fiction. Imposters? Yeah, they're dangerous. But I have every confidence that very soon the fake and the phony will give way to what's *really* dangerous: the real Jesus.

Because the only thing more dangerous than getting Jesus right . . . is getting Jesus wrong.

STUDY FAQS

This participant's guide is a companion to the six-session *Dangerous Jesus* video curriculum, available for online streaming at RightNow Media. You can also find out more at whoiskb.com. I recommend using this guide and the videos together for a study on your own, with your small group, or with a circle of friends that want to know the truth about who Jesus is and what Jesus stood for when He walked the earth.

Over the next six sessions, we'll explore the dangerous aspects of our Lord and our faith. We'll cover our dangerous Jesus, the dangerous gospel, dangerous love, dangerous community, dangerous blessing, and our dangerous identity.

The study is meant as a complement to my book, *Dangerous Jesus*. To maximize your experience, I suggest reading the book in full before beginning this study. However, the study will still be beneficial if you haven't made your way through *Dangerous Jesus* just yet.

My heart's desire for you in the coming weeks is that you'll come to know Jesus as the dangerous, countercultural, radical leader that He was. And along the way, I pray you'll also come to realize your own potential to be dangerously good in the Kingdom of God.

Here are some answers to FAQs to help get you started.

WHAT DO I NEED TO DO THIS STUDY?

To complete this study, you need this participant's guide, the book *Dangerous Jesus*, a Bible (or a Bible app on your phone), and the video sessions.

The book *Dangerous Jesus* takes an honest and indicting approach to the study of who Jesus really was during His time on earth and how we may have either gotten Him wrong or not gotten Him at all. I take a look at our interpretation of the gospel and how we may hold an incomplete version of the Good News. I also ask some tough questions about why most churches today look very different from the early church.

The videos serve to take you deeper into the content of *Dangerous Jesus* and help you personalize and apply some of the book's principles.

CAN I DO THIS STUDY ON MY OWN, OR DO I HAVE TO BE IN A SMALL GROUP SETTING?

As is the case with most topics of faith, unpacking our long-held beliefs may be a difficult task if done alone—difficult, but not impossible. We will do an entire session on the importance of dangerous friendships, and I recommend completing this study with at least one other person. Now, if you don't have anyone to complete this study with, you certainly can still participate. I'll be your partner, riding this journey with you.

I WANT TO LEAD A SMALL GROUP THROUGH THIS STUDY. HOW DO I GET STARTED?

First of all, good for you. Thank you for stepping up and leading the charge. If you aren't already plugged into a small group, I'd recommend starting with your friends first. "But KB," you might say, "my friends are wilding. My friends don't do the whole Jesus or church thing."

That's exactly who I wrote this study for.

I'd ask them just to show up for session 1 to see what they think. If they want to bounce after that, that's on them. But this isn't your typical Bible study. In fact, it's the opposite. This is a ruthless evaluation of the disparity between who the world thinks Jesus to be and who He really is.

The videos will do most of the legwork for you. Press play, then let Jesus do the rest. For more tips, see the "Tips for Leaders" section immediately following this one.

HOW LONG SHOULD EACH SESSION TAKE TO COMPLETE?

I'd carve out an hour for each session, including the time it takes to play the videos. Leave some time after the video to discuss any questions in this participant's guide that might benefit the group. If you're leading the group, I suggest preselecting which questions you'd like to raise.

Each session includes general questions, as well as five "at-home" days for participants to complete on their own. These entries should take about fifteen to twenty minutes to complete. Not only will they keep the introspection and conversation about our dangerous Jesus alive in your group's hearts and minds but they will also help you develop a consistent pattern of reading God's Word regularly (if that isn't your habit already).

All you need is access to a Bible and something to write with. There will be space in this participant's guide for you to write down your responses.

TIPS FOR LEADERS

First of all, you're a hero. Whether this is your first or your hundredth time leading a study, I'm thankful that you're answering the call to shepherd souls through this journey. I pray that as you lead this study, your faith will be multiplied exponentially.

Your main responsibility in leading is simply to stoke the fire of conversation that follows each video session. I'd also ask that you do the suggested reading prior to each session so your input is robust and aligned with the study.

If you're still a little unsure about how this should all go down, here's a few suggestions.

1. PUT IN THE WORK AHEAD OF TIME.

Coming prepared is the minimum requirement to successfully leading this study. Do the reading—and I mean *reading*. Skimming won't cut it in a study this complex. Take notes, jot down page numbers, underline quotes. If the room falls silent after the video plays, your legwork will be the difference maker in helping people open up and begin the discussion. Ideally, you'll have read the entire *Dangerous Jesus* book before the study starts.

I also recommend putting a star beside any of the group discussion questions you really want to cover. I've purposefully written more questions than you'll likely have time for to ensure a robust discussion.

2. BE VULNERABLE.

If you show up with your walls up, your group members are likely to follow in kind. You don't have to lead from your deepest, darkest secrets, but you may have to be the first one to share honestly.

3. STAY ON TOPIC.

It'll be tempting to share the latest scores and family updates, but try to keep the conversation focused on the study. If you have a particularly chatty group, plan fifteen to thirty additional minutes at the top of the study to catch up. But once the video starts playing, stay off the rabbit trails and on the road toward discovering a dangerous Jesus.

I'd also have a "share time" limit. Some group members may try to dominate the conversation. Placing a three-minute maximum on shares will keep the conversation moving.

4. DON'T WORRY IF YOU'RE NOT AN EXPERT.

Look, you don't need to be a Bible scholar to lead this study. All you need is to be willing to try. Saying, "I don't know, but I'll find out for you" is a sign not of weakness but of courage. No one has all the answers, and you don't have to either.

5. COMMIT TO PRAYING.

Pray for your group. Then pray some more. Prayer is a powerful tool that we have unlimited access to. Pray for your sessions. Pray that people's lives will be changed. Pray for your group members by name. And pray for yourself, asking God to give you His words and wisdom throughout the course of this study.

DANGEROUS JESUS

The only thing more dangerous
than getting Jesus right
is getting Jesus wrong.
***DANGEROUS JESUS*, CHAPTER 1**

ACTIVE LISTENING QUESTIONS

As you watch the video, listen for the answers to the following
questions. Jot down a few notes for each one.

1. Jesus puts anything that would stand against His
_____ _____ and our
_____ in danger.

2. What were the three ways the coming of Jesus was a threat to Caesar? He would
- out _____
- out _____
- out _____

3. Jesus' life was the embodiment of all that was good, true, and beautiful, and when He invades a world that is the opposite of all three, His very existence is what?

4. What three commands does Jesus ask of us?
1. _____ your enemy.
2. _____ to those who can't give back to you.
3. _____ in a way that is upside down.

5. How did Jesus show His dangerous love for us?

GROUP DISCUSSION QUESTIONS

Work through the following questions with your group. Make sure to leave enough time at the end to share prayer requests and spend a few minutes in prayer.

1. Before beginning your *Dangerous Jesus* journey, what words or phrases would you have used to describe Jesus?

2. Why do you think so many people struggle with the concept of a dangerous Jesus?

3. Rodney Stark, a sociologist of religion, lists three ways Jesus' ministry went from twelve disciples to millions of followers:[1]

   - People from different ethnic and social groups treated each other as family.

- Women were given higher social status and were allowed to lead in worship.
- Early Christians practiced radical hospitality toward one another and toward outsiders.

Of the three, which would have had the biggest influence on you choosing to follow Christ?

4. What do you think was the most countercultural message Jesus preached when He was on earth?

5. What does the following statement mean to you: "As Christians, each of us carries within us the potential to be dangerous"?

6. What is meant by the term "Christianity of the Land"? What evidence of its existence have you seen or experienced in your own life?

7. Chapter 1 of *Dangerous Jesus* describes many of the misrepresentations of Jesus. Which of these do you think is the most common?

- Is He ultra-right-wing Jesus, who spins a Christianity that is hostile toward the vulnerable and defensive of the powerful?
- Is He condemnation Jesus, who spins a Christianity that insists people know they are wrong without insisting they know they are loved?
- Is He patriot Jesus, who spins a Christianity that places America at the center of the universe, making the success of the United States tantamount to the success of God Himself?
- Is He weak Jesus, who spins a Christianity steeped in fear and fragility, consumed with threat-finding and a subsequent retreat from culture?
- Is He "vibes" Jesus, who spins a Christianity that is partner to our good time but never challenges us to be righteous?
- Is He winning Jesus, who spins a Christianity that associates the presence of God with success with little to say about suffering?

- Is He overspiritual Jesus, who spins a Christianity that scoffs at therapy, science, and any kind of "worldly" pleasure?

8. In Matthew 16:13-16, we read,

> When Jesus came to the region of Caesarea Philippi, he asked his disciples, "Who do people say that the Son of Man is?"
>
> They replied, "Some say John the Baptist; others, Elijah; still others, Jeremiah or one of the prophets."
>
> "But you," he asked them, "who do you say that I am?"
>
> Simon Peter answered, "You are the Messiah, the Son of the living God."

Now, how about you? Who do you say that Jesus is?

9. Chapter 1 of *Dangerous Jesus* says,

> This is precisely why so many of us think spirituality is merely doing our devotions every morning—just us and God. Devotions are important, but true religion—the religion God is pleased with—is demonstrated in action. Christianity is doing what Jesus did. He lived among us, loving, healing, and caring for others, along with teaching about His Kingdom.

> What would have to change about your life to make you more aligned with how Jesus lived His?

NOTE TO LEADERS

Close the session by asking if anyone has a specific prayer request to share with the group. Then lead the group in a prayer to close. You can also ask someone else in the group to lead the closing prayer.

DAY 1

At the end of the video session, I challenged you to consider a few questions. Write out your responses to these questions. Be brutally honest!

1. What makes me feel defensive?

2. What breaks my heart?

3. Where do I spend my time?

4. How do I use my money?

What do your answers to these questions reveal about who Jesus is in your life? Do you need to make any changes? If so, what?

DAY 2

Read John 5:16-22.

> The Jews began persecuting Jesus because he was doing these things on the Sabbath.
>
> Jesus responded to them, "My Father is still working, and I am working also." This is why the Jews began trying all the more to kill him: Not only was he breaking the Sabbath, but he was even calling God his own Father, making himself equal to God.
>
> Jesus replied, "Truly I tell you, the Son is not able to do anything on his own, but only what he sees the Father doing. For whatever the Father does, the Son likewise does these things. For the Father loves the Son and shows him everything he is doing, and he will show him greater works than these so that you will be amazed. And just as the Father raises the dead and gives them life, so the Son also gives life to whom he wants. The Father, in fact, judges no one but has given all judgment to the Son."

1. What is revealed about Jesus' relationship to God in this passage? How does that speak to how dangerous Jesus is?

2. John 14:12 records Jesus' words: "Truly I tell you, the one who believes in me will also do the works that I do. And he will do even greater works than these, because I am going to the Father."

   If we're to do "greater works than these," how does that speak to our own potential to be dangerous?

DAY 3

Read Jesus' words from Luke 6:20-36:

Then looking up at his disciples, he said:

Blessed are you who are poor,
because the kingdom of God is yours.
Blessed are you who are hungry now,
because you will be filled.

Blessed are you who weep now,
because you will laugh.
Blessed are you when people hate you,
when they exclude you, insult you,
and slander your name as evil
because of the Son of Man.

"Rejoice in that day and leap for joy. Take note—your
reward is great in heaven, for this is the way their
ancestors used to treat the prophets.

But woe to you who are rich,
for you have received your comfort.
Woe to you who are now full,
for you will be hungry.
Woe to you who are now laughing,
for you will mourn and weep.
Woe to you
when all people speak well of you,
for this is the way their ancestors
used to treat the false prophets.

"But I say to you who listen: Love your enemies, do what
is good to those who hate you, bless those who curse
you, pray for those who mistreat you. If anyone hits you
on the cheek, offer the other also. And if anyone takes
away your coat, don't hold back your shirt either. Give
to everyone who asks you, and from someone who takes
your things, don't ask for them back. Just as you want
others to do for you, do the same for them. If you love
those who love you, what credit is that to you? Even

sinners love those who love them. If you do what is good to those who are good to you, what credit is that to you? Even sinners do that. And if you lend to those from whom you expect to receive, what credit is that to you? Even sinners lend to sinners to be repaid in full. But love your enemies, do what is good, and lend, expecting nothing in return. Then your reward will be great, and you will be children of the Most High. For he is gracious to the ungrateful and evil. Be merciful, just as your Father also is merciful."

1. What is the most countercultural statement Jesus makes in this passage?

2. Which of the principles that Jesus discusses is the most challenging for you personally?

3. In order to be like our dangerous Jesus, what are three steps you can take *this week* to be more aligned with the Christianity He outlines in the passage above?

 i.

 ii.

iii.

DAY 4

Chapter 1 of *Dangerous Jesus* says,

> Dallas Willard used the term "vampire Christians" to describe those who say to Jesus, in essence, "I'd like a little of your blood, please. But I don't care to be your student or have your character. In fact, won't you just excuse me while I get on with my life, and I'll see you in heaven."[2]
>
> The blood of Jesus and what it affords us—eternal life and forgiveness of sin—are the essential perks of the package. But we try to bifurcate the perks of His blood from the person who shed that blood. In other words, we want what He can do for us, but we don't want to engage with what we are called to do through Him. It is of little benefit to have the words of Jesus in our mouths and not the ways of Jesus on our feet.

1. Why do you think so many Jesus followers have a "vampire Christian" mindset?

2. Have you ever been guilty of having Jesus' words in your mouth and not the ways of Jesus on your feet? Reflect on a few examples.

3. What does it look like to have the ways of Jesus on your feet in your day-to-day life?

DAY 5

Jesus was dangerous because He came as an affront to popular culture. His message was confounding—scandalous, even—to the religious leaders of His day. Jesus came as a light in the darkness, exposing things and people that had previously been in the shadows. He was a danger to danger because He brought love, compassion, and hope to *all* men and women—not just a select few.

1. On a scale from 1 to 10, how dangerous do you feel as a Jesus follower right now? Circle your response.

1   2   3   4   5   6   7   8   9   10

2. What are three ways you could increase your level of Christlike danger in the coming weeks?

    i.

    ii.

    iii.

DANGEROUS REFLECTION

Before you begin the next session, spend a few moments reflecting on what you've learned in session 1. Here are a few questions to reflect on.

1. How have I grown spiritually?

2. What new ideas have I embraced?

3. What have I learned about who Jesus *really* is?

4. What is one thing I *cannot* forget that I learned during this session?

DANGEROUS GOSPEL

The New Testament is not after converts.
The New Testament is after disciples.
***DANGEROUS JESUS*, CHAPTER 3**

BEFORE YOU BEGIN

Read chapters 3 and 4 of the Dangerous Jesus *book.*
Meet with your group and watch video session 2.

ACTIVE LISTENING QUESTIONS

As you watch the video, listen for the answers to the following
questions. Jot down a few notes for each one.

1. Two of the chief issues with the Christianity of the Land
are that its gospel is both _____ _____ and
also _____ _____ _____ .

2. The gospel is _____ in its scope, and it's also present in our _____. The gospel is invading right now, right here. It's a very _____ and _____ message.

3. What happens when the gospel gets busy?

4. When the gospel is just about your _____ _____, then it's just about you. That's a problem.

5. You can't expect a _____ _____ from a dangerous Jesus.

6. Jesus came to save the world but also to be a _____ in the darkness.

7. The dangerous gospel is not just introspective; it's _____, _____, and _____.

GROUP DISCUSSION QUESTIONS

Work through the following questions with your group. Make sure to leave enough time at the end to share prayer requests and spend a few minutes in prayer.

1. Are you a bad-news-first person? Or a good-news-first person? Explain the reasoning behind your preference.

2. Do you agree or disagree with the following statement: "Salvation alone is an incomplete gospel"? Explain your response.

3. In what ways has the gospel disrupted your life? If it hasn't, what does that communicate about your interpretation of the gospel?

4. Why do you think many churches today don't directly address issues like racism, police brutality, or abortion?

5. Why do you think the gospel of the American church has become so focused on converts?

6. Consider this verse from Micah 6:8 (esv):

> He has told you, O man, what is good;
>   and what does the Lord require of you
> but to do justice, and to love kindness,
>   and to walk humbly with your God?

With that Scripture in mind, do you believe you can be effective in the Kingdom of God without actively pursuing social justice? Explain your response.

7. Where do you have the biggest opportunity to share the dangerous gospel: at work, at home, or with friends? Is there someone in particular you can act on behalf of?

8. If we were to live more like Jesus, how would our day-to-day habits need to change?

9. In the past, have you been someone who agreed with the gospel or obeyed it? Explain your response.

NOTE TO LEADERS

Close the session by asking if anyone has a specific prayer request to share with the group. Then lead the group in a prayer to close. You can also ask someone else in the group to lead the closing prayer.

INDIVIDUAL STUDY

Participants are to complete the following questions on their own, ideally over the course of five different days. If there are any questions you didn't get to during the group discussion, you may want to work through them during the at-home study time.

DAY 1

Matthew 23:23-24 reads,

> Woe to you, scribes and Pharisees, hypocrites! You pay a tenth of mint, dill, and cumin, and yet you have neglected the more important matters of the law—justice, mercy, and faithfulness. These things should have been done without neglecting the others. Blind guides! You strain out a gnat, but gulp down a camel!

1. What are the "more important matters of the law" referenced in Matthew 23:23?

2. What is your first memory of hearing the gospel of Jesus Christ? How does that line up (or not) with Matthew 23:23?

3. Chapter 3 of *Dangerous Jesus* says,

In order to be a true threat to evil, the gospel must encompass redemption, justification, sanctification, salvation, and glorification. Not one of these pieces is the entirety of the gospel—all are interconnected. Whenever we make one of these things the entirety of the gospel, we lose the true scope, depth, and breadth of the gospel.

Which of the following has your gospel been about: redemption, justification, sanctification, salvation, or glorification?

4. Before session 2, how would you have described the gospel to someone else?

5. Has that description changed at all? Discuss why or why not.

DAY 2

Chapter 3 of *Dangerous Jesus* says,

> There is no such thing as a personal relationship with
> Christ that does not include personal care for others. . . .
> The gospel is a profoundly human message. I don't like
> using the popular church phrase "soul winning" because
> the Kingdom is not winning souls; it's winning *people*.
> The gospel is for human beings, which are bodies *and*
> souls. Jesus did not come to save half of you. He came to
> save all of you. The redemption of humankind, therefore,
> is the redemption of both body *and* soul. The gospel of
> the Kingdom always goes further.

1. Does your gospel include the personal care of others? If
not, how could you change that?

2. How does hearing that God came to redeem our souls
and our bodies affect the way we treat our bodies and the
way we view how others' bodies are treated?

3. Consider James's description of the dangerous gospel in James 1:27:

> Pure and undefiled religion before God the Father is this: to look after orphans and widows in their distress and to keep oneself unstained from the world.

What does James say is "pure and undefiled religion"? How does that align with your perception of American Christianity?

DAY 3

Read the following Scriptures:

> I am not ashamed of the gospel, because it is the power of God for salvation to everyone who believes, first to the Jew, and also to the Greek. For in it the righteousness of God is revealed from faith to faith, just as it is written: The righteous will live by faith.
>
> ROMANS 1:16-17

> We ought to thank God always for you, brothers and sisters loved by the Lord, because from the beginning God has chosen you for salvation through sanctification by the Spirit and through belief in the truth. He called

you to this through our gospel, so that you might obtain the glory of our Lord Jesus Christ. So then, brothers and sisters, stand firm and hold to the traditions you were taught, whether by what we said or what we wrote.

2 THESSALONIANS 2:13-15

Calling the crowd along with his disciples, he said to them, "If anyone wants to follow after me, let him deny himself, take up his cross, and follow me. For whoever wants to save his life will lose it, but whoever loses his life because of me and the gospel will save it. For what does it benefit someone to gain the whole world and yet lose his life? What can anyone give in exchange for his life? For whoever is ashamed of me and my words in this adulterous and sinful generation, the Son of Man will also be ashamed of him when he comes in the glory of his Father with the holy angels."

MARK 8:34-38

1. What do these Scripture passages teach us about the full, dangerous gospel?

    a. Romans 1:16-17

    b. 2 Thessalonians 2:13-15

c. Mark 8:34-38

2. In session 2 we learned that preaching the gospel means overcoming the works of the enemy wherever they are found. Societal injustice is not a side issue. A gospel that does not care about societies is not the gospel at all. What are some societal issues that interest you? What is one step you can take *today* to overcome the works of the enemy as it relates to that issue?

DAY 4

Listen to what John 12:44-46 says:

> Jesus cried out, "The one who believes in me believes not in me, but in him who sent me. And the one who sees me sees him who sent me. I have come as light into the world, so that everyone who believes in me would not remain in darkness."

The light doesn't need light. The darkness does. Your light is needed in the dark rooms of pain, evil, oppression, sin, and marginalization.

1. Which statement is more accurate to your life? *I am most often a light in a room of lights.* Or *I am most often a light in a room of darkness.*

2. Why do you think many Christians struggle to find "rooms of darkness" to shine their light in?

3. What is the potential benefit to others when you shine your light in a room full of darkness? What is the potential benefit to *you*?

DAY 5

In Matthew 19:16-28, we read the story of the rich young ruler:

> Just then someone came up and asked him, "Teacher, what good must I do to have eternal life?"
>
> "Why do you ask me about what is good?" he said to him. "There is only one who is good. If you want to enter into life, keep the commandments."

"Which ones?" he asked him.

Jesus answered: Do not murder; do not commit adultery; do not steal; do not bear false witness; honor your father and your mother; and love your neighbor as yourself.

"I have kept all these," the young man told him. "What do I still lack?"

"If you want to be perfect," Jesus said to him, "go, sell your belongings and give to the poor, and you will have treasure in heaven. Then come, follow me."

When the young man heard that, he went away grieving, because he had many possessions.

Jesus said to his disciples, "Truly I tell you, it will be hard for a rich person to enter the kingdom of heaven.

Again I tell you, it is easier for a camel to go through the eye of a needle than for a rich person to enter the kingdom of God."

When the disciples heard this, they were utterly astonished and asked, "Then who can be saved?"

Jesus looked at them and said, "With man this is impossible, but with God all things are possible."

Then Peter responded to him, "See, we have left everything and followed you. So what will there be for us?"

Jesus said to them, "Truly I tell you, in the renewal of all things, when the Son of Man sits on his glorious throne, you who have followed me will also sit on twelve thrones, judging the twelve tribes of Israel."

1. How do you or don't you relate to the rich young ruler?

2. What was the rich young ruler's interpretation of the gospel?

3. Why is it hard for someone who is rich to enter the Kingdom of Heaven?

4. Ultimately, what do we learn about the dangerous gospel from this passage? How can you apply that lesson in your daily life?

DANGEROUS REFLECTION

Before you begin the next session, spend a few moments reflecting on what you've learned in session 2. Here are a few questions to reflect on.

1. How have I grown spiritually?

2. What new ideas have I embraced?

3. What have I learned about who Jesus *really* is?

4. What is one thing I *cannot* forget that I learned during this session?

DANGEROUS LOVE

We will never be conservative enough, liberal enough, or woke enough to be truly at home in any of the world's circles.
***DANGEROUS JESUS*, CHAPTER 4**

BEFORE YOU BEGIN

Read chapters 5 and 6 of the Dangerous Jesus *book.*
Meet with your group and watch video session 3.

ACTIVE LISTENING QUESTIONS

As you watch the video, listen for the answers to the following questions. Jot down a few notes for each one.

1. The Bible says in Matthew 6:21, "Where your treasure is, there your _____ will be also."

2. If we _____ people who are gifted and popular but never _____ people who aren't gifted and popular, what does that say about our _____?

3. The Christianity of _____ identifies greatness according to a person's love for _____.

4. A willingness to bear someone else's burdens and a willingness to lay down our lives for our friends is the very

_____ ____ _____ _____.

5. One of the primary ways we worship God is through _____ _____ and service to our _____.

6. Loving our enemies does not mean we excuse them. But it does mean that we should posture ourselves for _____, pray for their _____, and not refuse them _____ if the opportunity arises.

GROUP DISCUSSION QUESTIONS

Work through the following questions with your group. Make sure to leave enough time at the end to share prayer requests and spend a few minutes in prayer.

1. What's your response to the question "What does the Lord require of me?"

2. If what and who we elevate reveals what and who we value, where are our values as a society?

3. How do you think our values line up with what Jesus values? How do you think the people we elevate line up with who Jesus elevated? How do you think our hearts line up with Jesus' heart?

4. Scripture says, "For the mouth speaks from the overflow of the heart" (Matthew 12:34). I would add, "For the comments section speaks from the overflow of the heart." How do our online comments relate to Jesus' command to love our neighbor with a dangerous love?

5. The first question people typically ask in matters of justice is "What do we do?" But dangerous love teaches us that we should first ask, "Who is God?" How might the answer to the latter question inform our response to the first?

6. What applications could the story of the Good Samaritan have for the stories of George Floyd, Breonna Taylor, and Ahmaud Arbery?

7. Matthew 22:34-39 says,

> When the Pharisees heard that he had silenced the Sadducees, they came together. And one of them, an expert in the law, asked a question to test him: "Teacher, which command in the law is the greatest?"
>
> He said to him, "Love the Lord your God with all your heart, with all your soul, and with all your mind. This is the greatest and most important command. The second is like it: Love your neighbor as yourself."

Jesus gives not one but two commandments: love God with everything you've got, and love other people the way you love yourself. When Jesus says, "The second is like it," He is basically saying, "What I am about to say is inextricably connected to the thing I just said." Does the American church place the same emphasis on loving God and loving others? Explain your response.

8. How are mercy and justice related in Scripture? How are they related (or not) in the church?

9. Chapter 5 of *Dangerous Jesus* says,

> Do not be afraid to hear the observations of people outside the faith community (Samaritans) on how society is failing its vulnerable people. Respect the image of God enough to believe victims can honestly share their victimization without knowing Jesus. Go do justice.
>
> There will inevitably be places where you agree with BLM, critical race theorists, and even socialists. Do not fear that your faith is now in jeopardy because someone you perceive as an ideological opponent has a good (or better) point. All truth is God's truth, and it will be in these truth intersections that we find windows to proclaim the excellency of Christ!

What "truth intersections" have you encountered over the course of the last three sessions? How will you respond?

NOTE TO LEADERS

Close the session by asking if anyone has a specific prayer request to share with the group. Then lead the group in a prayer to close. You can also ask someone else in the group to lead the closing prayer.

INDIVIDUAL STUDY

Participants are to complete the following questions on their own, ideally over the course of five different days. If there are any questions you didn't get to during the group discussion, you may want to work through them during the at-home study time.

DAY 1

Chapter 4 of *Dangerous Jesus* says,

> When Jesus taught the disciples how to pray in Matthew 6, He instructed them to call for God's "will [to] be done on earth as it is in heaven" (Matthew 6:10). Jesus made it clear that our primary function in this world is to bring heaven down. We do this by seeking to transform the world in a way that represents the ethics and the reality of the Kingdom of God. This is why we take justice seriously. This is why we take protecting the unborn seriously. This is why we take feeding the hungry and caring for the poor seriously. This is why we take treating the immigrant with respect seriously. This is why we want to see reform in politics that goes beyond Democrats and Republicans to a Kingdom ethic.
>
> Jesus was constantly challenged to give His support to the conservative Pharisees, the liberal Sadducees, or the imperial Romans. All of them got *some* of His support, but none of them got *all* of His support. No nation's agenda is large enough to encompass the agenda of the Kingdom citizen.
>
> If your wagon is hitched to Jesus, you will inevitably

find yourself agreeing, intersecting, and aligning with all kinds of movements and political camps as you travel through this world. But rest assured, at some point, Jesus is going to complicate things and possibly get you kicked out!

1. Do you think politics are connected to your spiritual walk? Why or why not?

2. How does our country's bipartisan dynamic align with Jesus' actions and allegiances while on earth?

3. Have you experienced any political confusion while following Jesus?

4. Can you admit one thing about your political party that you aren't fully in agreement with?

5. If you were to align your politics more directly to Jesus' priorities, what would have to change?

DAY 2

Jesus says that we shouldn't worry about who our neighbors are in order to draw circles around who we don't have to value and love. Instead, we are to concern ourselves with *being* loving neighbors to whoever around us is in need. *That* is what it means to love God.

1. According to Jesus, who are your neighbors? Think:

- community
- statewide
- nationwide
- globally

2. If anyone in need is to be considered a neighbor, how can we realistically and intentionally show them the dangerous love of Jesus?

DAY 3

The greatest examples of faith and godliness among us are not necessarily the gifted articulators or the students with deep theological training. They are not necessarily the well-followed celebrity pastors and speakers. They are not necessarily the prophets of our congregations. No. According to Jesus, the greatest examples of faith among us are those who love greatly.

1. Who is someone you know who loves greatly? How do they carry themselves? How do they speak? What motivates their decisions?

2. Do you consider yourself to be someone who loves greatly? Give evidence to support your response.

3. What are three loving acts you can intentionally plan and execute over the next thirty days? Be realistic! I want you to truly embrace the idea that we are never more in love with our Savior than when we're loving the people He created.

   i.

   ii.

   iii.

DAY 4

Read the following Scripture passages:

> The LORD is gracious and righteous;
> our God is compassionate.
> The LORD guards the inexperienced;
> I was helpless, and he saved me.
> PSALM 116:5-6

> Your compassions are many, LORD;
> give me life according to your judgments.
> PSALM 119:156

> Therefore the LORD is waiting to show you mercy,
> and is rising up to show you compassion,
> for the LORD is a just God.
> All who wait patiently for him are happy.
> ISAIAH 30:18

1. Based on these Scriptures, what is God's posture toward justice?

2. Do you share God's posture? How or how not?

3. How can you love more dangerously according to these Scriptures?

DAY 5

Chapter 4 of *Dangerous Jesus* says,

> Brothers and sisters, we will never be conservative enough, liberal enough, or woke enough to be truly at home in any of the world's circles. There is only one place where we are truly at home, and that is in God's Kingdom. But it is precisely our dual citizenship that should make us the unsung assets of whatever spaces we find ourselves in, because we can speak both inside and outside of those camps with transcendental truths.

Our bias should be to righteousness. That's our only dog in the fight. Just like loving God over people makes us better lovers of people, so too does being a good citizen of heaven make you a better citizen of this world.

1. Do you ever experience the tension of having a "dual citizenship"? Explain your response.

2. How does our dual citizenship qualify us to be assets in the spaces we find ourselves in?

3. What would have to change for your bias to be righteousness?

4. What are a couple of ways you could love dangerously, becoming a better citizen of the world?

DANGEROUS REFLECTION

Before you begin the next session, spend a few moments reflecting on what you've learned in session 3. Here are a few questions to reflect on.

1. How have I grown spiritually?

2. What new ideas have I embraced?

3. What have I learned about who Jesus *really* is?

4. What is one thing I *cannot* forget that I learned during this session?

DANGEROUS COMMUNITY

The church has to be more than simply
an answer to loneliness in our culture,
because God designed the church to be
the answer to the loneliness in our culture.
***DANGEROUS JESUS*, CHAPTER 7**

ACTIVE LISTENING QUESTIONS

As you watch the video, listen for the answers to the following
questions. Jot down a few notes for each one.

1. Generation Z has been called the _____ generation
   to ever live.

2. We *need* _____ to thrive on this earth.

3. What is the biblical Greek word for the type of bond we're supposed to share with other Christians? (Don't worry—no one's gonna check your spelling!)

4. Proverbs 18:1 says, "One who _____ himself pursues selfish desires; he rebels against all sound wisdom."

5. One of the first characteristics of a good dangerous church is that it encourages _____.

6. Our identities are found in _____, not our failures.

7. What is the second aspect of true community?

GROUP DISCUSSION QUESTIONS

Work through the following questions with your group. Make sure to leave enough time at the end to share prayer requests and spend a few minutes in prayer.

1. Did you experience an increase or decrease of loneliness during the COVID-19 pandemic? What circumstances contributed to that?

2. Do you tend to be an isolator or a connector? What factors from your past have contributed to your social wiring?

3. Why do you think it's more difficult to make friends as an adult than it was when we were kids?

4. How does social media give a false sense of community? Have you ever experienced positive community on social media?

5. What makes Jesus the GOAT of friendship?

6. Why do you think the modern church isn't our automatic answer to our loneliness?

7. I cannot overstate how spiritually risky it is to aim to be a Christian by yourself. Why do you think so many people end up doing just that?

8. How do you see evidence of God's relational nature in the creation narrative?

9. In Ephesians 3:10, Paul says, "This is so that God's multi-faceted wisdom may now be made known through the church to the rulers and authorities in the heavens." If you were to look at the unity within the church right now, does it express the "multi-faceted wisdom" of God? If not, what does it express?

NOTE TO LEADERS

Close the session by asking if anyone has a specific prayer request to share with the group. Then lead the group in a prayer to close. You can also ask someone else in the group to lead the closing prayer.

DAY 1

Chapter 7 of *Dangerous Jesus* says,

> Jesus reveals the importance of Christian community in His final words before going to the cross. Knowing that His time on this earth is coming to a close, Christ chooses to spend His last moments talking about community. People's last words typically carry the weight of their legacy, and what is on Jesus' mind? His friends. Christ's prayer is that the church would "be one, as you, Father, are in me and I am in you. May they also be in us" (John 17:21). Brothers and sisters, there you have it. Jesus' last words before His brutal death are a prayer that the bond of unity that exists in the Godhead would be present in His people. The Creator of the universe exists in a friendship. From eternity, the Father, Son, and Spirit have existed together in perfect harmony, unity, and yes, friendship. Who do you think created the concept?

1. What is your general attitude toward friendships?

2. Is it shocking to you that these were Jesus' last words before His murder? Why or why not?

3. What is good-dangerous about the way Jesus approached fellowship and community? Why do you think this kind of community has such power?

4. Knowing that Jesus was in a good-dangerous community, do you feel that building a dangerous community of your own should be a priority? How have you invested (or could you invest) in building one?

DAY 2

Proverbs 11:14 says,

> Without guidance, a people will fall,
> but with many counselors there is deliverance.

1. Where do you seek guidance? Who are your advisers?

2. When was the last time you genuinely sought advice from a God-fearing community? Did you follow it? What happened?

3. Why is it human nature to try to figure it out on our own?

4. Is it enough to have one Christian friend we can rely on? Use Scripture to support your response.

DAY 3

Read the following Scripture references:

The one who walks with the wise will become wise, but a companion of fools will suffer harm.
PROVERBS 13:20

Do not be deceived: "Bad company corrupts good morals."
1 CORINTHIANS 15:33

1. Think through your friend group. How many of your relationships are "friendships of convenience"? (A friendship of convenience means you're friends because life has somehow put you together versus a friendship you intentionally sought out for their wisdom and character.)

2. Have you ever experienced the truths outlined in the two Scripture passages above? What happened?

3. Are there any friendships you have now that may be lessening your impact in the Kingdom of God? How can you address that?

4. How can you pursue the type of biblical community I talked about in our session together—a dangerous community where you can "walk in the light"?

DAY 4

1 Peter 4:8 says,

> Above all, maintain constant love for one another, since love covers a multitude of sins.

1. On a scale of 1 to 10, what is your comfort level with saying "I love you" to your closest friends? Circle your response.

   1   2   3   4   5   6   7   8   9   10

2. Why does the word *love* make some people uncomfortable within the context of friendship?

3. Read John 13:1:

   Before the Passover Festival, Jesus knew that his hour had come to depart from this world to the Father. Having loved his own who were in the world, he loved them to the end.

   Who did Jesus call His "own"? How did He love them? Was it a love in word alone?

4. If our dangerous Jesus was able to admit His unending love for His friends, even going so far as to wash their feet, how should we conduct our own dangerous friendships? What example did Jesus set for us?

DAY 5

Chapter 7 of *Dangerous Jesus* says,

> One of the reasons our friendships are often so shallow is because we won't walk in the light that's necessary to deepen them. But you are only as close to somebody as the extent to which you are willing to be vulnerable with them, even when it's messy. If I can parrot Pastor Ray Ortlund one more time, he says, "You can be impressive, or you can be known. But you can't be both."[1] Make it look like you've got it all together or enter into deep relationship with God and others—you can't have both.

1. Would you rather be known or impressive? Do your actions reflect your response?

2. Do you agree with Pastor Ray Ortlund's statement "You can impressive, or you can be known. But you can't be both"? Explain your response.

3. If we readily acknowledge that we are all sinners, why is it so difficult for us to confess our sins to one another?

4. Read James 5:16:

> Confess your sins to one another and pray for one another, so that you may be healed. The prayer of a righteous person is very powerful in its effect.

According to James, why do we confess our sins to each other? What is the benefit?

5. Can you identify someone (or a group of people) that you would be comfortable sharing your sins with regularly? If not, would that be something you'd ever be open to doing? Why or why not?

1. How have I grown spiritually?

2. What new ideas have I embraced?

3. What have I learned about who Jesus *really* is?

4. What is one thing I *cannot* forget that I learned during this session?

DANGEROUS BLESSING

What we find in the living God is not the end of happiness but the source of happiness.
***DANGEROUS JESUS*, CHAPTER 9**

BEFORE YOU BEGIN

Read chapters 9 and 10 of the Dangerous Jesus *book. Meet with your group and watch video session 5.*

ACTIVE LISTENING QUESTIONS

As you watch the video, listen for the answers to the following questions. Jot down a few notes for each one.

1. Our problem is that we only see the hand of God working when things are neat, resolved, and explainable—when things fall perfectly into place for
_____ _____.

2. We are looking up to heaven saying, "Who will show us some _____? When will the _____ _____ come?"

3. We have to recognize that better times don't begin when our _____ ends. Better times begin when the _____ _____ _____ is near to us.

4. When the presence of God has become necessary for us to make it through, God has _____ us up.

5. Many of us are caught up in the gospel of _____.

6. The fruit of _____ is the presence of God, not necessarily the presence of God's _____.

7. The problem with the Christianity of the Land is that it cares more about _____ than it does about transformation.

8. What is our inheritance from God?

GROUP DISCUSSION QUESTIONS

Work through the following questions with your group. Make sure to leave enough time at the end to share prayer requests and spend a few minutes in prayer.

1. During this session, I talk about the birth of my daughter, Nala. What I thought was an injustice by God turned out to have the trickle-down effect of dangerous blessings. Have you ever had a similar experience?

2. Can you relate to David's words in Psalm 4:6 (ESV): "Who will show us some good?" What about your life or the world today prompts you to ask that question?

3. Have you ever considered that there may be something better than an end to our suffering? How does that idea make you feel? How does it explain some of your past wounds?

4. According to the Bible, who is blessed among us?

5. I think all of us accept the idea that there will be suffering in this life. After all, even our King Jesus suffered! So why is it that when we suffer, we are tempted to question the goodness of God?

6. What is meant by the phrase "Our joy is only God-deep"?

7. Why is it easier for us to imagine Jesus healing the sick and raising the dead than it is for us to imagine Him laughing with His friends or crying in the garden of Gethsemane?

8. Have you ever experienced or witnessed God using tragic circumstances as a spiritual accelerant?

9. How can we reframe the deep societal and personal losses of recent years to be more aligned with the truth of God's dangerous blessings?

NOTE TO LEADERS

Close the session by asking if anyone has a specific prayer request to share with the group. Then lead the group in a prayer to close. You can also ask someone else in the group to lead the closing prayer.

DAY 1

Many Christians struggle because they live their lives trying to deny their humanity. But the truth is, we weren't made for heaven—we were made for earth. We were made intentionally human. Yes, heaven is the intermediary place believers go to as we await the second coming of Jesus. But after that, our ultimate destination is the new earth, where we will live as glorified humans.

1. Why do you think Christians expend so much energy denying their humanity?

2. We can't find Jesus' bones, leading us to the realization that when He ascended into heaven, He went in His human body. What does that tell us about our humanity?

3. Not only did God provide us with senses but He also formed us with interests. He gave us minds that love strategy, sports, and science. He gave us hands to sculpt, hold children, and create. How does the way God created us inform how we view both our humanity and the earth around us?

DAY 2

Chapter 9 of *Dangerous Jesus* says,

One of the greatest threats to the Christianity of Christ is the misguided belief that following Jesus means giving up every conceivable earthly pleasure in the name of piety. The problem with that is too often people believe that not only should we be resisting evil, we should equally be resisting good. Though there is great power in controlling our appetites, giving up the good things we enjoy does not always equal nearness to God. I've spent a lot of time in this book talking about decentering self, but I do not want to overlook God's call to be instructed on how to love your neighbor by considering the way you love yourself (see Mark 12:31). Self-love is good as long as it doesn't stop at self or permit the evil that self might desire. If in the name of loving God we refuse to love ourselves by enjoying good things, we are literally cutting ourselves off from a whole world of experiences that were meant to nourish our faith and increase our love for God.

1. Have you ever felt like in order to be a good Christian, you have to live without pleasure? Where do you think that idea comes from?

2. What does God mean in Mark 12:31 when He commands us to love our neighbors as ourselves?

3. In a culture where self-love is promoted on virtually every platform, what do you think it means to love oneself in a biblical sense?

4. Do you think Jesus practiced self-love? Explain your response using Scripture references.

5. How do you practice self-love? Do you think the way you love yourself matters to God?

DAY 3

Read Jesus' prayer from John 17:6-19:

> I have revealed your name to the people you gave me from the world. They were yours, you gave them to me, and they have kept your word. Now they know that everything you have given me is from you, because I have given them the words you gave me. They have received them and have known for certain that I came from you. They have believed that you sent me.
>
> I pray for them. I am not praying for the world but for those you have given me, because they are yours. Everything I have is yours, and everything you have is mine, and I am glorified in them. I am no longer in the world, but they are in the world, and I am coming to

you. Holy Father, protect them by your name that you have given me, so that they may be one as we are one. While I was with them, I was protecting them by your name that you have given me. I guarded them and not one of them is lost, except the son of destruction, so that the Scripture may be fulfilled. Now I am coming to you, and I speak these things in the world so that they may have my joy completed in them. I have given them your word. The world hated them because they are not of the world, just as I am not of the world. I am not praying that you take them out of the world but that you protect them from the evil one. They are not of the world, just as I am not of the world. Sanctify them by the truth; your word is truth. As you sent me into the world, I also have sent them into the world. I sanctify myself for them, so that they also may be sanctified by the truth.

1. Judging by Jesus' words in this prayer, what did He mean by "the world"?

2. What does it mean to be "in the world"?

3. You may have heard the Christian maxim "In the world, not of it." Why do Christians sometimes focus on not being "of the world" to the point that they forget that they were designed to be "in the world"?

4. What would it look like for you to be "in the world" in a biblical way?

DAY 4

In Psalm 19:1-3, David wrote,

The heavens declare the glory of God,
and the expanse proclaims the work of his hands.
Day after day they pour out speech;
night after night they communicate knowledge.
There is no speech; there are no words;
their voice is not heard.

1. When was the last time you paused to find joy in creation?

2. How does God's handiwork in creation "pour out speech" and "communicate knowledge"?

3. If the heavens and skies could actually speak, what do you think they would say about their Creator? Do we say those things about the One who created us?

4. If possible, spend some time outside or looking out a window. Behold the expansive heavens—the colors, the depth, the glory. Write down what you see, what you feel, what you discern about our Creator.

DAY 5

The great C. S. Lewis said,

> We can ignore even pleasure. But pain insists upon being attended to. God whispers to us in our pleasures, speaks in our conscience, but shouts in our pains: it is His megaphone to rouse a deaf world. . . . No doubt pain as God's megaphone is a terrible instrument; it may lead to final and unrepented rebellion. But it gives the only opportunity the bad man can have for amendment. It removes the veil; it plants the flag of truth within the fortress of the rebel soul.[1]

1. What did Lewis mean by the phrase "We can ignore even pleasure"? Is that true for you?

2. Why does God often choose the megaphone of pain as His means for a dangerous blessing?

3. What "flags of truth" have been planted in your soul by God?

4. Do you think you can grow in your faith at the same rate in the absence of suffering?

5. First Peter 2:19-21 says,

> It brings favor if, because of a consciousness of God, someone endures grief from suffering unjustly. For what credit is there if when you do wrong and are beaten, you endure it? But when you do what is good and suffer, if you endure it, this brings favor with God.
>
> For you were called to this, because Christ also suffered for you, leaving you an example, that you should follow in his steps.

What does it mean to suffer "for good"? What is the example Christ set for us in suffering? How can that change the way we view our suffering today?

6. What is something you are going through right now that may be a dangerous blessing? Are you willing to view the presence of God as a gift and not an injustice?

Before you begin the next session, spend a few moments reflecting on what you've learned in session 5. Here are a few questions to reflect on.

1. How have I grown spiritually?

2. What new ideas have I embraced?

3. What have I learned about who Jesus *really* is?

4. What is one thing I *cannot* forget that I learned during this session?

DANGEROUS IDENTITY

What the enemy wants to do is convince us that God isn't who He says He is and that we aren't who God says we are.
***DANGEROUS JESUS*, CHAPTER 12**

BEFORE YOU BEGIN

Read chapters 11 and 12 of the Dangerous Jesus *book. Meet with your group and watch video session 6.*

ACTIVE LISTENING QUESTIONS

As you watch the video, listen for the answers to the following questions. Jot down a few notes for each one.

1. It is the enemy's ultimate goal to convince us of two things: one, that God isn't actually who He says He is, and two, _____

_____.

2. When the Lord opened my eyes to His glory, His power, and His goodness, I quickly realized that the competitive edge for Christianity was not the cool stuff. The cool stuff was _____ _____.

3. God is the origin of _____.

4. _____ who God is—and _____ you are who He says—is the only way to outmaneuver the enemy when it comes to our _____.

5. If God is good and His image is in us, then His _____ is on us. If God is courageous and strong and His image is on us, that gives us access to _____ and _____. That's who we are. If God is powerful and His image is in us, we are people of _____ in Him.

6. If we are in Him, then ultimately we are the dangerous
_____ of the dangerous _____.

GROUP DISCUSSION QUESTIONS

Work through the following questions with your group. Make sure
to leave enough time at the end to share prayer requests and spend
a few minutes in prayer.

1. How would you describe the identity of God?

2. Have you ever had your financial identity hijacked? How
do we (as a society) behave when our financial identities
have been hijacked through credit card fraud or a similar
circumstance? How do we (as Christians) behave when
our spiritual identities have been hijacked?

3. How has Satan attacked our identity as individuals? As
Christians? As a country?

4. When others don't see our value, how does that feel? How do we react? How *should* we react?

5. What messages have you received about your identity over the course of your life? Think about the words and actions of others that linger. How have these occasions affected the way you view yourself?

6. Is your life a reflection of *who* you are or *whose* you are? What's the difference?

7. Are you living like you're good? Like you're brave, powerful, and dangerous? In what ways?

8. Do you believe you can be as dangerous as Jesus? Do you want to be as dangerous as Jesus? What would that look like?

9. How would the world around us look different if we were to live as dangerously as Jesus?

10. How would you describe your personal identity? Do you live like you are a powerful, beloved, dangerous child of God? If not, why? What's stopping you from living out your dangerous identity?

NOTE TO LEADERS

Close the session by asking if anyone has a specific prayer request to share with the group. Then lead the group in a prayer to close. You can also ask someone else in the group to lead the closing prayer.

INDIVIDUAL STUDY

Participants are to complete the following questions on their own, ideally over the course of five different days. If there are any questions you didn't get to during the group discussion, you may want to work through them during the at-home study time.

DAY 1

First John 2:3-11 says,

> This is how we know that we know him: if we keep his commands. The one who says, "I have come to know him," and yet doesn't keep his commands, is a liar, and the truth is not in him. But whoever keeps his word, truly in him the love of God is made complete. This is how we know we are in him: The one who says he remains in him should walk just as he walked.
>
> Dear friends, I am not writing you a new command but an old command that you have had from the beginning. The old command is the word you have heard. Yet I am writing you a new command, which is true in him and in you, because the darkness is passing away and the true light is already shining. The one who says he is in the light but hates his brother or sister is in the darkness until now. The one who loves his brother or sister remains in the light, and there is no cause for stumbling in him. But the one who hates his brother or sister is in the darkness, walks in the darkness, and doesn't know where he's going, because the darkness has blinded his eyes.

1. How do we demonstrate that we know Jesus?

2. What is the new command given in this Scripture passage?

3. Can you keep this new command and still have unforgiveness in your heart toward your brother or sister?

4. Is there someone you have unforgiveness toward right now? If appropriate, describe the situation and how you feel about it.

5. Are you willing to embrace your dangerous identity, offering forgiveness so you can live in the light? If so, write a quick prayer here, asking God to help you forgive. Stop stumbling around in the dark—release your offender.

DAY 2

The first five books of the Bible detail a cosmic introductory class written by Moses and presented to the newly founded people of God. The Hebrews had been enslaved for years. No doubt, their identity had become their oppression. And still, God had chosen this small group of slaves to be His people. After explaining the miraculous and marvelous way God created the universe and everything in it, Moses says in Genesis 1:26-27,

> God said, "Let us make man in our image, according to our likeness. They will rule the fish of the sea, the birds of the sky, the livestock, the whole earth, and the creatures that crawl on the earth."

So God created man
in his own image;
he created him in the image of God;
he created them male and female.

1. What is the significance in who God chose to be His people?

2. What was Moses trying to communicate to the people
   when he told them how God created them? Why might
   that have been especially important for the Hebrew slaves
   to hear?

3. What does it mean to you that you were created in the
   image of God? What words would you use to describe
   who God is? Do you believe those same qualities are
   innately and inextricably in you too?

4. How should the knowledge of who God is affect our identity? How should it affect the way we live? The way we interact with others? The way we feel about ourselves?

5. How can you shift your current perspective of your identity to be more in line with the truth that you are a reflection of a dangerous God?

DAY 3

The words *Jesus* and *humility* are synonymous. But as humans, we struggle to be Christlike in this area. There is a draw to pride, to self-promotion, to defensiveness in all of us.

Chapter 12 of *Dangerous Jesus* says,

Since our engagement with culture and in our communities prohibits us from blocking out the voices around us, we must develop reflexes or disciplines that make us discerning. One of the keys, I think, to staying centered in who God wants us to be is our pursuit of humility. The pursuit of humility is not being overly sensitive to criticism or overly dependent on praise. Ultimately, the praise that matters the most is "Well done, good and faithful servant" (Matthew 25:23). You can get all kinds of praise from all kinds of people, but if you do not get that one commendation from the One who created you, the rest of it doesn't matter. But if we put God's praise first, above all others, we won't have to question our identity, and criticism will not sink us.

1. How would you define humility? How did Jesus define it (with His actions and His words)?

2. Do you tend to be more sensitive to criticism or more overly dependent on praise?

3. What do you think is required to one day hear your Father say the words "Well done, good and faithful servant"? Use Scripture references in your response.

4. What would it look like for you to put God's praise first?

DAY 4

Above all else, the identity of a Christian is love. Lovers are danger-ous, because love is what this world stands most in need of.

1. How has Christ expressed His love for you?

2. How do you express your love for others?

3. How does a Christian walk the often indiscernible line between sharing truth and sharing love?

DAY 5

In *The Weight of Glory*, C. S. Lewis writes,

> It is a serious thing to live in a society of possible gods
> and goddesses, to remember that the dullest and most
> uninteresting person you can talk to may one day be a
> creature which, if you say it now, you would be strongly
> tempted to worship, or else a horror and a corruption
> such as you now meet, if at all, only in a nightmare.
> All day long we are, in some degree, helping each other
> to one or other of these destinations. It is in the light
> of these overwhelming possibilities, it is with the awe
> and the circumspection proper to them, that we should
> conduct all our dealings with one another, all friendships,
> all loves, all play, all politics.[1]

1. Toward what destination are you steering the people in
your life? In other words, are you living as a threat to
good or a threat to evil?

2. How could you better leverage your dangerous identity to
be part of the solution and not the problem?

1. How have I grown spiritually?

2. What new ideas have I embraced?

3. What have I learned about who Jesus *really* is?

4. What is one thing I *cannot* forget that I learned during this session?

WRAPPING UP

As we conclude this study together, I give you credit. You've read the book. You've watched the videos. And you've asked yourself hard questions. All those steps require time, money, and intentionality—dangerous intentionality.

I fervently pray that your eyes and heart have been opened to who Jesus really is and what He is really about. I pray the truth of His dangerous spirit has seeped into your spirit and that it has emboldened you to walk in the light of what He says is true, good, and right.

Above all else, I pray you have been filled with awe by the lavish and ridiculous nature of His unending love for you, His image-bearing child. I pray that same love fills you to the brim and runs over, splashing across the pages of the story God is writing with your life.

NOTES

SESSION 1: DANGEROUS JESUS
1. Quotes are from Keas Keasler, "Ethics & Spiritual Formation," presented at Arise City Summit, Tampa, FL, June 23, 2018. They are based on Rodney Stark, *The Rise of Christianity: How the Obscure, Marginal Jesus Movement Became the Dominant Religious Force in the Western World in a Few Centuries* (San Francisco: HarperSanFrancisco, 1997).
2. Dallas Willard, *The Great Omission: Reclaiming Jesus's Essential Teachings on Discipleship* (New York: HarperCollins, 2006), 14.

SESSION 4: DANGEROUS COMMUNITY
1. Ray Ortlund (@rayortlund), "You can be impressive, or you can be known. But you can't be both," Twitter, November 19, 2018, 6:16 a.m., https://twitter.com/rayortlund/status/1064477525093568514.

SESSION 5: DANGEROUS BLESSING
1. C. S. Lewis, *The Problem with Pain* (San Francisco: HarperOne, 2001).

SESSION 6: DANGEROUS IDENTITY
1. C. S. Lewis, *The Weight of Glory* (United Kingdom: HarperCollins, 2001), 45–46.

ABOUT THE AUTHOR

Kevin "KB" Burgess is a Dove Award–winning rapper, speaker, and podcaster. With four full-length albums to his name—including 2020's *His Glory Alone*, for which he won the Dove Award for Rap/Hip-Hop Album of the Year—the multi-hyphenate artist is an inimitable force on today's scene. He has become a number one hitmaker and has received critical acclaim for his studio releases with placement on *Billboard*'s Top 200 Album Chart and top 5 on *Billboard*'s Top Rap Album Chart.

KB blends the creative and the pastoral with ease, having carved a unique space for himself as a hip-hop and worship experimentalist. His refined rawness conveys a kind of victory-lap energy you can't help but feel in your bones. One such example is "Church Clap," the bass-heavy rally cry that went Gold.

KB is cohost of the popular podcast *Southside Rabbi*. The podcast features in-depth conversations on art, theology, and current events and boasts hundreds of thousands of downloads per week across multiple platforms. Furthermore, HGA—a movement he spearheaded made up of multiethnic, urban men and women from all walks of life—has amassed a loyal following around the globe.

Although KB wears many hats, the joy of being a husband to Michelle and a father to their three children holds his heart and continues to propel him into the man God wants him to be.

Visit him online at whoiskb.com.

THE DANGEROUS JESUS EXPERIENCE

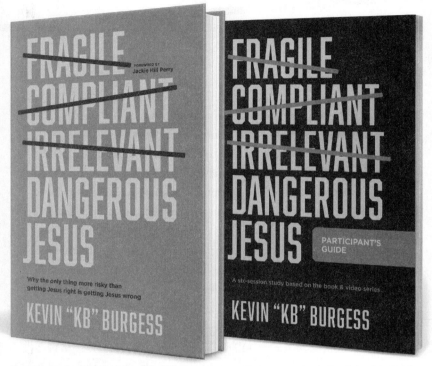

Dangerous Jesus: Why the Only Thing More Risky than Getting Jesus Right Is Getting Jesus Wrong

Dangerous Jesus Participant's Guide: A Six-Session Study Based on the Book and Video Series

COMPANION STREAMING VIDEO SERIES
AVAILABLE THROUGH RIGHTNOW MEDIA

Available everywhere books are sold.

www.whoiskb.com

CP1907